IT'S ALL IN THE
PACKAGE:
PAID IN FULL

IT'S ALL IN THE PACKAGE:
PAID IN FULL

Apostle Para D. Knight

IT'S ALL IN THE
PACKAGE:
PAID IN FULL

IT'S ALL IN THE
PACKAGE:
PAID IN FULL

IT'S ALL IN THE PACKAGE: PAID IN FULL

Copyright © 2023 by Apostle Para D. Knight

All rights reserved. This book or parts thereof may not be stored in a retrieval system, reproduced in any form, or transmitted in any form by any means

Mechanical, photocopy, electronic, recording, or otherwise without prior written permission of the author, except as provided by United States of America copyright law.

ISBN: 978-1-934905-31-9

Printed in the United States of America

IT'S ALL IN THE
PACKAGE:
PAID IN FULL

IT'S ALL IN THE PACKAGE:
PAID IN FULL

DEDICATION

This book is dedicated to my mother, the late Reeda Mae Stephens-Holmes who I love and who I also tribute my success! She blessed me so, I never wanted for anything growing up!

This book is dedicated to the late Apostle Retha M. Wells-Daniel who was a big sister, my second mother, my mentor, my confidant, my cheerleader, and my best friend. You are missed, but never forgotten.

This book is also dedicated to my sister the late Barbara Stephens, we had some awesome times together.

Love You Always, Sister!

I also dedicate this book to my son and daughter, Ramon Clark & Nicole Clark who

I love dearly. You both are a blessing to me.

Also, I dedicate this book to my sister, Patricia Stephens and my big brother, Larry Stephens.

Last but not least, I dedicate this book to new believers and to those who have been walking this Christian journey, continue to go forth!

Apostle Para D. Knight

ACKNOWLEDGEMENTS

First and foremost, I want to thank GOD for His GRACE & MERCY, FAITH, and HOLY SPIRIT who enabled me to step out and write this book!

My friend Pastor Sandra Carter, Dr. Clovice Collins, Prophetess Donna Figgs, and finally, my ram in the bush, Apostle Charissee Lewis, when I told her my book had been out in the middle of the ocean for about 4 ½ years she said, "Ok let's bring it to shore!"

Also, I acknowledge Kingdom Konnectors, an awesome team of people, that have been a part my journey!

THANKS EVERYBODY!

FORWARD

In this book, IT'S ALL IN THE PACKAGE: PAID IN FULL Apostle Para D. Knight goes deep into the word of God, and shows keys on how to defeat the enemy. Apostle Para D. Knight exposes the enemy and gives strategies to equip new believers to be victorious in the midst of opposition. She also ignites believers who have been in the faith for a while to reacquaint themselves in the word of God. You will enjoy this book, as Apostle Para D. Knight shares personal experiences, prophetic fulfillment, and miraculous testimonies of how God showed up and showed out on her behalf!

Apostle Para D. Knight, thank you for allowing Worldwide Kingdom Publishing to publish your book. We look forward to working with you again for there are many more books within you!

In His Service,

Dr C. Lewis

IT'S ALL IN THE
PACKAGE:
PAID IN FULL

TABLE OF CONTENTS

Dedication

Acknowledgements

Forward

Chapter One
Major Key to Receiving the Package 11

Chapter Two
Results of Not Fully Applying Yourself to Reading the Word 18

Chapter Three
Keeping A Balance & Paying Attention.......29

Chapter Four
Receiving 39

Chapter Five
Big Secret 48

Chapter Six
Grace 56

Chapter Seven
Wisdom, Knowledge & Understanding 64

Chapter Eight
Constantly Renewing Your Mind 72

Chapter Nine
The Faith of Jesus Brings Manifestation ...80

Chapter Ten
The Truth Will Make You Free 90

Chapter Eleven
God is Faithful: Testimony Time 97

Ending Scriptures To Study.................105

Chapter One

MAJOR KEY TO RECEIVING THE PACKAGE

Do you own a master key? Have you ever needed a master key to open all doors? God has given us keys to use in the spiritual realm according to **{KJV} {Matthew 16:19}** "And I will give unto thee the Keys of the Kingdom of heaven: and whatsoever thou shalt bind on earth shall be bound in heaven: and whatsoever thou shalt loose on earth shalt be loosed in heaven." So according to scripture, God has given us the Keys to the Kingdom to gain access to enter into the spiritual realm. The keys that God has given us are superior to anything in the universe. Keys give us access to everything that is in the PACKAGE of God that is why I say, everything that we need pertaining to life and godliness we have already received.

Therefore, the major key to receiving the PACKAGE which is God's written word [the logos] is believing in Jesus Christ. The scripture tells us,

{AMP} {Romans 10:9, 10} "Because if you acknowledge and confess with your mouth that Jesus is Lord [recognizing His power, authority, and majesty as God], and believe in your heart that God raised Him from the dead, you will be saved." "For with the heart a person believes in Jesus Christ as Savior resulting in his justification that is; being made righteous, being freed of the guilt and shame and made acceptable to God; and with the mouth you acknowledge and confess, your faith in Him openly, resulting in and confirming your salvation."

In conclusion reader, in order to receive the PACKAGE you must open your mouth and declare your belief and trust in God, by acknowledging that Jesus Christ is Lord!

Please answer the following questions:

{1}. How would you go about obtaining the keys of the kingdom?

_____

_____

_____

_____

{2}. How would you appropriate or apply the keys in your life?

_____

_____

_____

_____

_____

IT'S ALL IN THE
PACKAGE:
PAID IN FULL

{3}. Do you believe you can apply that to any situation in your life? (yes or no)

_____

_____

{4}. Identify areas in your life where you need to apply the master key:

_____

_____

_____

_____

{5}. How would you apply the key in everyday life?

_____

_____

_____

_____

IT'S ALL IN THE
PACKAGE:
PAID IN FULL

{6}. Now that you have the key and PACKAGE, how will you share with others that they too, may have victory in their lives?

_____

_____

_____

{7}. How will you share with others the knowledge you received from reading the PACKAGE?

_____

_____

_____

_____

_____

IT'S ALL IN THE
PACKAGE:
PAID IN FULL

{8}. What inspired you to pick up the PACKAGE?

_____

_____

_____

_____

{9}. Now that you know you have the authority of binding and loosing, how will you use this authority?

_____

_____

_____

_____

IT'S ALL IN THE
PACKAGE:
PAID IN FULL

{10}. Release your faith and demonstrate your authority, by writing what you have learned?

_____

_____

_____

_____

_____

_____

_____

_____

_____

Chapter Two

RESULTS OF NOT FULLY APPLYING YOURSELF TO READING THE WORD

Do you know how important it is for a believer to read the word of God? I will use an example of a new born baby: if you do not feed the baby naturally; the baby will be unnourished, and will die from starvation. As it is in the natural; so it is in the spiritual! We must eat the whole roll: the word of God from Genesis to Revelation. Another example is yourself, if you do not feed yourself natural food, you will die of starvation. It works the same way in the spirit realm. If you do not feed your spiritual man; he can become spiritually weak and starve from spiritual malnutrition. When the spirit man is not connected to God and insulated with the word of God, you can become spiritually dead. Therefore, when trials and tribulations arises in your life; you will have no stamina to stand or be strong to resist your enemy, the devil!

Results From Applying Myself

In my early walk with Christ, I did not apply myself whole heartily in reading the word of God. I would read a little here and there; until the Holy Spirit showed me an illustration of a free-standing lamp plugged in with a 40-watt bulb not screwed firmly in the socket. Because the bulb was not screwed in completely, the light would flicker on and off. That was me with my bible sitting on the table; sometimes open, but the majority of the time, closed. You could say I was a part-time reader. Once I screwed the light bulb all the way in the socket tightly, the light stayed on continuously, but it was dim because it was only a 40-watt bulb. However, the more I applied myself in the word of God: the 40-watt became a 60-watt. As I increased by reading more of the word of God, the 60-watt became a 100-watt, and the 100-watt became a 150-watt. Eventually, the 150-watt became a flood light. I was enlightened by reading the word of God and it became a seed. The seed of the word was planted in me and it began to germinate and grow. As the seed grew stronger, it was producing understanding, truth, knowledge, revelation, and wisdom within me. The word of God began to illuminate inside of me. The light of God's word became brighter as I continued to read and study His word. The more I read, my faith began to grow. As it grew within me, I started thriving and flourishing. I began to trust more in what the Holy Spirit told me and show me through revelation. The more I read the word, it caused me to stand and become unmovable and unshakable as I went through trials and tribulations. He also began speaking to me in dreams, in prayer, and it caused me to open my mouth to prophesy, regularly. Quickly, many prophetic words materialized in the lives of individuals. I saw part of people's destinies completed. For example, I saw in the spiritual realm, my sister graduating from nursing school in her cap and gown; walking across the stage, despite her failure and struggle with her grades. God did it!

I also saw, a major hospital in Michigan close down, from God's prophetic word; but many people who I warned prophetically did not believe it. However, God's word came to pass. Know this, warning always comes before destruction. Also, God showed me a famous car dealership would closed down in Michigan, and it did. The Lord led me to prophesy to one of the employee's that he would need to find new employment and the prophetic word came to pass.

Also, I remembered in the early 80's, my husband at the time, which is now my ex-husband was laid off from the Ford Motor Plant. He was told that he would never return or come back to any Ford Motor Plant in Michigan. My faith through prayer in God showed me different. During that time, he was transferred from Flatrock, Michigan Ford Motor Plant to Sharonville, Ohio where there was no hope of him returning to a Ford Motor Plant in Michigan. But low and behold, through trusting God in this matter; it caused my ex-husband and I to see a different outcome, regardless of what man said. He was brought back to the Ford Motor Plant in Livonia, Michigan. During those years in the plant, racism was at an all time high; but if God has to bless thousands of people because of one person to fulfill His promise, He will do it.

As you can see through my walk with God, it has caused me to trust God, more and more on this journey. My eyes have been enlightened since my heart was opened to see and my ears was opened to hear.

{KJV} {Ephesians 1:17, 19} "That the God of our Lord Jesus Christ, the Father of glory, may give unto you the spirit of wisdom and revelation in the knowledge of him:"

"The eyes of your understanding being enlightened; that ye may know what is the hope of his calling, and what the riches of the glory of his inheritance in the saints, and what is the exceeding greatness of his power to us-ward who believe, according to the working of his mighty power."

{NIV} {2 Thessalonians 1:3} "We ought always to thank God for you, brothers, and sisters, and rightly so, because your faith is growing more and more, and the love all of you have for one another is increasing."

{KJV} {Romans 1:17} "For therein is the righteousness of God revealed from faith to faith: as it is written, the just shall live by faith."

Please answer the following questions:

{1}. Do you take time to read your word?

_____

_____

{2}. How often do you read your word? (Explain)

_____

_____

_____

IT'S ALL IN THE
PACKAGE:
PAID IN FULL

{3}. How often do you surround yourself with Christians or unbelievers?

_____

_____

{4}. What areas in your life that need to be perfected by the word of God? {please list}

_____

_____

_____

_____

{5}. How important is the word of God to your walk?

_____

_____

{6}. How often do you meditate on God's word and study to be quiet in His presence?

_____

_____

_____

_____

{7}. How often do you speak the word of God out of your mouth?

_____

_____

_____

_____

IT'S ALL IN THE PACKAGE: PAID IN FULL

{8}. Your words can make you or break you; but speaking the word of God, will give you good success in life. Have you been speaking the word of God over your life? Share your scriptures:

_____

_____

_____

_____

{9}. Do you have a prayer life?

_____

_____

_____

_____

_____

_____

IT'S ALL IN THE
PACKAGE:
PAID IN FULL

{10}. Are your prayers effectual and fervent, according to **{KJV} {James 5:16}**?

_____

_____

_____

_____

_____

_____

_____

_____

_____

_____

Chapter Three

KEEPING A BALANCE & PAYING ATTENTION

Are you balanced in your walk with God? The word of God says in {**KJV**} {**Proverbs 11:1**} "A false balance is an abomination to the Lord: but a just weight is his delight." As Christians, it is important to build our lives on the right foundation, which is the word of God. I am reminded of the scriptures in the word of God {**KJV**} {**Matthew 7:24, 25, 26, 27**} "Therefore whosoever heareth these sayings of mine, and doeth them, I will liken him unto a wise man, which built his house upon rock:" "And the rain descended, and the floods came, and the winds blew, and beat upon that house; and it fell not: for it was founded upon a rock." "And every one that heareth these sayings of mine, and doeth them not, shall be likened unto a foolish man, which built his house upon the sand:"

"And the rain descended, and the floods came, and the winds blew, and beat upon that house; and it fell: and great was the fall of it." The enemy is a watcher and listener. The things you do not pay attention to, he does. It's a two way street; he is watching the way you are looking and reacting to trials and tribulations in your life. He is listening to what you are speaking out of your mouth negatively to ambush you. He knows automatically, a person who is not standing or trusting, and believing in the word of God. The scripture says, **{NIV} {I Peter 5:8}** "Be alert, and of sober mind. Your enemy the devil prowls around like a roaring lion looking for someone to devour." So you see the importance of paying attention. It can spare you from going through unwarranted battles in life.

About eight years ago or longer, God spoke to me and said, "DIVINE HEALTH."

IT'S ALL IN THE PACKAGE: PAID IN FULL

These words had never been spoken personally to me. I heard it and I did not pay attention to it. I continued to eat the wrong foods, and I was not paying attention to my health. I was very distracted by marital issues which kept me stressed and unfocused with the things of God. It also caused an imbalance in my life as a whole. Well, let me share a little of my spiritual history. During a certain period in my life, I was mostly going by prophetic words in my life. Let me explain, words spoken to me by God's Prophets or prophetic men and women of God. I must confess, at that time, I was being lazy about getting into the word of God for myself, big mistake! You must read and meditate on God's word for yourself, and do not rely on others to do it for you. I am not knocking prophecy, for I am a Prophet myself, and I love the prophetic. It is essential not to become a prophetic junkie. You cannot get in the habit of relying on prophecy, alone.

{KJV} {I Corinthians 14:3} "But he that prophesieth, speaketh unto men to edification, and exhortation, and comfort." We can see according to scripture prophecy alone, is not enough to build a foundation. It does not replace reading the bible which is God's written word the (logos). We must keep a balance and never rely on prophetic words alone, because the word of God is the final authority!

{KJV} {Hosea 4:6} "My people are destroyed for lack of knowledge: because thou hast rejected knowledge, I will also reject thee, that thou shalt be no priest to me: seeing thou hast forgotten the law of thy God, I will also forget thy children." So now that God has sent Jesus Christ in the new covenant, Jesus and the word are one and because you have accepted Him you can have access to everything in the PACKAGE.

IT'S ALL IN THE PACKAGE: PAID IN FULL

{KJV} {2 Timothy 2:15} "Study to shew thyself approved unto God, a workman that needed not to be ashamed, rightly dividing the word of truth." This scripture is in reference to everything you have read in this chapter. When we study we receive knowledge, understanding, revelation, illumination, and information.

{KJV} {John 10:27} "My sheep hear my voice, and I know them, and they follow me:" By being in prayer and communing with God, this establishes a personal intimate relationship with God, where you will know His voice.

{KJV} {Joshua 1:8} "This book of the law shall not depart out of thy mouth; but thou shalt meditate therein day and night, that thou mayest observe to do according to all that is written therein: for then thou shalt make thy way prosperous, and then thou shalt have good success."

IT'S ALL IN THE
PACKAGE:
PAID IN FULL

Please answer the following questions:

{1}. Please elaborate what you have gained from reading this chapter:

_____

_____

_____

_____

{2}. Examine your relationships, observe to see if anyone is causing an imbalance to divert your walk:

_____

_____

_____

IT'S ALL IN THE PACKAGE: PAID IN FULL

{3}. Who are you drawn to that has a great influence on your life?

_____

_____

_____

_____

_____

{4}. How much time do you spend with negative people during the course of the day?

_____

_____

_____

_____

IT'S ALL IN THE
PACKAGE:
PAID IN FULL

{5}. Thus far in your life, what principles have you built your life on?

_____
_____
_____
_____
_____

{6}. What bad experiences have you built your life on?

_____
_____
_____
_____
_____

IT'S ALL IN THE
PACKAGE:
PAID IN FULL

{7}. What experiences in your childhood have affected the way you have built your life?

_____

_____

_____

_____

_____

{8}. Who or what has been the biggest deterrence in your life?

_____

_____

_____

_____

IT'S ALL IN THE PACKAGE: PAID IN FULL

{9}. What places have you visited or been that has caused a negative effect in your life?

_____

_____

_____

_____

{10}. Whom or what have influenced you to go overboard which caused you not to focus and pay attention to the instructions of God's word?

_____

_____

_____

_____

Chapter Four

RECEIVING

First of ALL, hold on to your healing YOU ARE HEALED! Hold on at all cost! Be ye steadfast and unmovable holding on in ALL things. Hold on to the profession of your FAITH. For we know that the enemy, the devil, has a plan to steal from you what you have already received from God through His Son, Jesus Christ. So, let me elaborate on some of his tactics. Not only concerning your healing; but with everything that pertains unto life and godliness that God has given us. One of the absolute signs that you have received your healing or any other things pertaining to life and godliness; the continued harassment of the enemy. The enemy systematically, begins to whisper in your ear, immediately. He says things like "You are not healed, don't you still feel the pain or symptoms, or don't you see nothing has changed, in your current situation." He will even start to magnify the demonic symptoms which I call lying, false, deceptive symptoms. I want to also include these other areas that he will try to deceive you in your life. Not only your healing, and your overall health; but it could also be in your finances, family, wealth, marriage, ministry, business, job, and children. You name it and the enemy will lie. He will tell you, your victory is not going to happen. You must not change the profession of your faith. You must remember your healing is already done! It is finished, according to the words of Jesus Christ when He hung on the cross and said, "It is finished!" If it is healing that you received or your prayers being answered or a prophetic word you received concerning your healing, or anything else; stand on His word.

So, you see my brothers and sisters it is more than just being healed. It is divine health, divine life, divine wealth it is being made whole in EVERY area of your life! SPIRIT, SOUL, and BODY.

{KJV} {John 10:10} "The thief cometh not, but for to steal, and to kill, and to destroy: I am come that they might have life, and that they might have it more abundantly."

{KJV} {3 John 1:2} "Beloved, I wish above all things that thou mayest prosper and be in health, even as thy soul prospereth."

{KJV} {2 Peter 1:3} "According as his divine power hath given unto us all things that pertain unto life and godliness, through the knowledge of him that hath called us to glory and virtue:"

{KJV} {1Peter 2:24} "Who his own self bare our sins in his own body on the tree, that we, being dead to sins, should live unto righteousness: by whose stripes ye were healed.

They ALL go hand and hand. GLORY BE TO GOD! It's all included in the PACKAGE. There are also other benefits not only for you but for your entire family in this great PACKAGE!

{AMP} {Acts 16:31} "And they answered, "Believe in the Lord Jesus as your personal Savior and entrust yourself to Him and you will be saved, you and your household [if they also believe]

{ESV} {Acts 2:38, 39} "And Peter said to them, Repent and be baptized every one of you in the name of Jesus Christ for the forgiveness of your sins, and you will receive the gift of the Holy Spirit." "For the promise is for you and for your children and for all who are far off, everyone whom the Lord our God calls to himself."

IT'S ALL IN THE
PACKAGE:
PAID IN FULL

Please answer the following questions:

{1}. Choose 2 scriptures from this chapter write what they mean to you?

_____

_____

_____

_____

{2}. What are the things in your life that you believe that has hindered you or stopped you from receiving God's promises?

_____

_____

_____

{3}. Do you believe that anything can stop you from receiving the things of God? Yes_____ or No _____

IT'S ALL IN THE
PACKAGE:
PAID IN FULL

{4}. Whatever your answer was in question 2 explain to the best of your knowledge based on your answer above.

_____

_____

_____

{5}. Are you open and willing to receive the GOOD NEWS that's ALL IN THE PACKAGE?

_____

_____

{6}. Name some areas in your life where the enemy of this world has blinded you or kept hidden from you, your purpose and destiny in life:

_____

_____

_____

IT'S ALL IN THE
PACKAGE:
PAID IN FULL

{7}. Do you believe that God wants you and your entire family to receive the best, spiritually and naturally?

_____

_____

_____

_____

{8}. What is your remedy or plan now to eradicate lack in ALL areas of your life?

_____

_____

_____

_____

_____

IT'S ALL IN THE PACKAGE: PAID IN FULL

{9}. What are your weakest areas in receiving from God?

_____

_____

_____

_____

_____

_____

_____

_____

_____

_____

IT'S ALL IN THE PACKAGE: PAID IN FULL

{10}. What bad advice have you received to stop you from going forward? (who, what, where, when, and how)

_____

_____

_____

_____

_____

_____

_____

_____

_____

Chapter Five
BIG SECRET

Let me share with you a big secret that the devil does not want you to know. He wants to rob you of your FAITH in believing what God has said and already done for you, by getting you caught up in your feelings. What I mean by this, is that he knows that you are use to operating out of your five natural senses, which I list them below:

SIGHT

TASTE

SMELL

HEARING

TOUCHING

The secret things belong to the Lord, but as you being a born again believer, you have the ability to tap in. You have the ability to tap into the supernatural realm of God that is not revealed to your natural senses.

IT'S ALL IN THE
PACKAGE:
PAID IN FULL

THE HOLY SPIRIT REVEALS UNKNOWN THINGS TO THE NATURAL MIND

Because I am a spirit filled born again believer, the Holy Spirit began to speak things to me I had not read before. Some might say, how could that be? It is because of the Holy Spirit that dwells in me, He knows ALL THINGS! You were in the mind of Christ before you were formed in your mother's belly. So the Holy Spirit will reveal to you secret things, just as He revealed to me.

{TLB} {Ephesians 1:4, 11} "Long ago, even before he made the world, God chose us to be his very own through what Christ would do for us; he decided then to make us holy in his eyes, without single fault- we who stand before him covered with his love." "Moreover, because of what Christ has done, we have become gifts of God that he delights in, for as part of God's sovereign plan we were chosen from the beginning to be his, and all things happen just as he decided long ago."

{TLB} {John 16:13} "When the Holy Spirit, who is the truth, comes, he shall guide you into all truth, for he will not be presenting his own ideas, but will be passing on to you what he has heard. He will tell you about the future."

{KJV} {1Corinthians 2:10, 11, 12} "But God hath revealed them unto us by his Spirit: for the Spirit searched all things, yea, the deep things of God." "For what man knoweth the things of a man, save the spirit of man which is in him? even so the things of God knoweth no man, but the Spirit of God."

"Now we have received, not the spirit of the world, but the spirit which is of God; that we might know the things that are freely given to us of God."

Please answer the following questions:

{1}. Reflect on what the above scriptures mean to you?

_____

_____

_____

_____

_____

_____

_____

_____

IT'S ALL IN THE PACKAGE: PAID IN FULL

{2}. What do you desire that is good from God that you have not seen in the natural realm yet?

_____

_____

_____

_____

{3}. What are the things that you have imagined and dreamed about that is positive?

_____

_____

_____

_____

IT'S ALL IN THE
PACKAGE:
PAID IN FULL

{4}. Where have you been a failure at in your life? Now that you have gained information from reading the PACKAGE how will you change your life?

_____

_____

_____

_____

_____

{5}. How important do you see the reading of God's word?

_____

_____

_____

_____

_____

IT'S ALL IN THE PACKAGE: PAID IN FULL

{6}. What has God shared with you in prayer that has been a secret, thus far?

_____

_____

_____

_____.

{7}. Now that you received the PACKAGE can you birth your prayer secret from the invisible realm in to the visible realm?

_____

_____

_____

_____

{8}. Do you like to bless, encourage, edify, counsel, comfort, and instruct others?

_____

_____

_____

_____

{9}. Are there hidden talents in you?

_____

_____

{10}. What do you think are your strongest gifts and talents?

_____

_____

Chapter Six
GRACE

As my journey continues, I know IT'S ALL IN THE PACKAGE. I have found out and I'm still finding out that it has a great benefit called GRACE & MERCY. They work hand and hand together. Frankly speaking readers, Grace is receiving good not because you are good, but just because God loves us. We can not earn His good or His blessings: for instance, you receive something good that you know you did not deserve, that's Grace and Favor. Grace sees you flawless, through the eyes of God. Grace is also not going to hell for all the wrong you have done. Grace is an enabler to help you do what you are called to do in life. It also helps you to do what you could not do in your own ability, such as: write a book, start a business, and be a good husband or wife these are just a few things mentioned, there are so much more. Another powerful example of Grace is when you receive compassion when you have not shown compassion for others. Mercy is a blessing of divine favor. An example of Mercy is a person is speeding in a no speeding zone; the speed limit is 70 mph, and the police officer pulls you over, for driving 85 mph and does not give you a ticket. In other words, Mercy is receiving a pass when you know you deserved the punishment!

I found out this PACKAGE contains more than keeping you out of hell and fire insurance; it contains so much more. Are you not excited? As I continue to emerge myself in God's word, I discovered more good news about GOD'S AMAZING GRACE! Not only did we receive a great PACKAGE, but GRACE has already provided everything for us, in this life and after. It is not based on how good we are or what we can work for in our own self efforts, but simply through His Son JESUS CHRIST, who died on the cross for our sins and trespasses, the debt is PAID IN FULL! We are getting GOOD THINGS not because we are good; but because He is GOOD. We are receiving things we do not deserve; because He PAID the price and took our penalties. It should have been me or you nailed to the cross to suffer for our sins, but He did so, that we could have a great benefit PACKAGE that we have received, through his GRACE & MERCY.

You see, GRACE said "YES!" MERCY said, "YES, we will take the punishment for them!"

ACQUITTED NOT GUILTY!

{KJV} {Romans 4:16} "Therefore it is of faith, that it might be by grace; to the end the promise might be sure to all the seed; not to that only which is of the law, but to that also which is of faith of Abraham; who is the father of us all."

{KJV} {Galatians 3:13} "Christ hath redeemed us from the curse of the law, being made a curse for us: for it is written, Curse is everyone that hangeth on a tree:"

{KJV} {Ephesians 2:8, 9} "For by grace are ye saved through faith; and that not of yourselves: it is the gift of God:" "Not of works, lest any man should boast."

Please answer 10 questions concerning Grace & Mercy:

{1}. What does grace and mercy mean to you in your own words?

_____

_____

_____

IT'S ALL IN THE
PACKAGE:
PAID IN FULL

{2}. What have you ever received that was good that you know, you really didn't deserve it?

_____

_____

_____

{3}. Who do you know in this world that would die for all your wrong doings?

_____

_____

{4}. Who do you know in this world that would deem you as perfect, flawless no matter how messed up you are?

_____

_____

IT'S ALL IN THE
PACKAGE:
PAID IN FULL

{5}. How many people do you know in this world that will cancel an insurmountable debt for you and your family, no matter how unworthy you are ?

_____

_____

{6}. How many people do you know that would burn and go to hell for you, and your family?

_____

{7}. How many people do you know that no matter how you have mistreated them, lied on them, and been unmerciful to them that will still love you and show mercy to you, and do good by you?

_____

_____

IT'S ALL IN THE
PACKAGE:
PAID IN FULL

{8}. Based on reading IT'S ALL IN THE PACKAGE: can you name a person or persons who loves you with all your faults, ugly ways, and all your flaws and loves you beyond measure?

_____

_____

_____

_____

{9}. Have you been able to do something you were not qualified to do or been on a job interview where they only hired by race and you were not the right race they preferred; but you were hired anyway?

_____

_____

_____

IT'S ALL IN THE
PACKAGE:
PAID IN FULL

{10}. Have you ever received healing and you knew you opened the door for the sickness and disease?

_____

_____

We have so much to be grateful for; that we did not qualify for, God's grace, mercy, and favor has given us a new outlook on life. It has caused our eyes to be enlighten and our hearts opened. It has also increased us to know all things are possible to them that believe in Him!

{KJV} {Jude:1:24, 25}

"Now unto to him that is able to keep you from falling, and to present you faultless before the presence of his glory with exceeding joy." "To the only wise God our Saviour, be glory and majesty, dominion and power, both now and ever." Amen.

Chapter Seven

WISDOM, KNOWLEDGE, AND UNDERSTANDING

Now, I am really on a quest for more knowledge, wisdom, and understanding of God's plan for my life. My insides were ecstatic at this point and I am still excited about this journey. You may also be on a quest and journey in your life as you are reading this book. As I continue my quest and journey, I found out that I have more relatives in the spirit realm that I did not know. I have a sister by the name of Wisdom, and cousins by the name of Knowledge, and Understanding. Wisdom is the solution to long standing problems that we can not solve in our natural thinking. It is an answer to your problems. It is tapping into the supernatural wisdom of God to receive His instructions and directions to confront and solve lingering issues.

Knowledge is revelation, information, and facts about a subject you was clueless of and unable to grasp. Knowledge is also the Holy Spirit revealing truth in areas in which you lacked spiritual and natural comprehension. Prophetically, knowledge is also revealing your past, present, and future. Lastly, understanding is the ability to perceive in clarity the things that are revealed to the natural mind. It is a deeper concept that you have received truth.

Do you want to know how I found out about wisdom, understanding, and knowledge? By reading the word of God, and researching different translations of the Bible.

{KJV} {Joshua 1:8} "This book of the law shall not depart out of thy mouth; but thou shalt meditate therein day and night, that thou mayest observe to do according to all that is written therein: for then thou shalt make thy way prosperous, and then thou shalt have good success."

{KJV} {Proverbs 1:20, 23} "Wisdom cried without; she uttereth her voice in the streets". "Turn you at my reproof: behold, I will pour out my spirit unto you, I will make known my words unto you."

{KJV} {Proverbs 2:6} "For the LORD giveth wisdom: out of his mouth cometh knowledge and understanding."

{NKJV} {Proverbs 7:4} "Say to wisdom, "You are my sister," "And call understanding your nearest kin."

IT'S ALL IN THE
PACKAGE:
PAID IN FULL

Please answer the following questions on wisdom, knowledge, and understanding:

{1}. Have you ever received instructions on how to do and what to do that you had no knowledge of at all?

_____

{2}. What is wisdom?

_____

_____

_____

_____

{3}. How would you apply the word of wisdom to your life?

_____

_____

_____

IT'S ALL IN THE
PACKAGE:
PAID IN FULL

{4}. What is the opposite of wisdom?

_____

_____

{5}. How do you obtain wisdom to solve problems in your life, naturally or spiritually?

_____

_____

_____

_____

{6}. Name two other principles that accompany wisdom:

_____

_____

_____

IT'S ALL IN THE
PACKAGE:
PAID IN FULL

{7}. Who do you go to spiritually or naturally to resolve a problem?

_____

{8}. If you lack wisdom, where is that scripture found in the PACKAGE?

_____

_____

_____

_____

{9}. Do you believe the wisdom of God supersedes all human wisdom?

_____

_____

_____

IT'S ALL IN THE
PACKAGE:
PAID IN FULL

{10}. Why would you ask God for wisdom?

___

___

___

___

___

___

___

___

___

___

IT'S ALL IN THE
PACKAGE:
PAID IN FULL

*Reflect back on what you read in this chapter, and share what you learned:

_____

_____

_____

_____

_____

_____

_____

_____

_____

_____

Chapter Eight

CONSTANTLY RENEWING YOUR MIND

Have you ever experienced a mental battle by being oppressed in your mind? This oppression affected your thinking and your ability to believe what you knew was right. It seemed to be contrary to the word of God. It caused you to always second guess yourself or doubt; when normally you had no problem with your confidence. Also, it caused you to doubt the prophetic words God had spoken to you. When you have experienced trauma the mind seems to keep you stagnated and stuck in the past; even though, there is something better for you in your future. The mind is the area where the enemy attacks to keep you distracted from achieving your purpose in life. Therefore, this is why it is so important to have the mind of Christ and a healthy mind. The natural mind is ineffective or futile when it comes to understanding the plan of God for your life. Your mind must constantly be renewed by the word of God. By sowing the seed of God's word into the inner man, your mind will begin to combat and destroy negative thinking; because your inward parts desire inner truth. Faith is essential to the renewal of the mind; because it causes you to hope, and dream outside of the normal box. The normal box only confines you to your 5 natural senses. Thinking outside of the normal box will take you to a place in the realm of your faith where your 5 natural senses has never gone before. You see, in your normal box you don't think or go beyond the perimeters of that box where you are only use to operating in your 5 natural human senses. It will take you to unfamiliar territory, a place unknown to humanity. It will also take you to a place that is invisible to the natural eye; but seen in the spiritual. A place you dreamed about; but thought you could never achieve in life. Faith has no boundaries, it is a blank canvas that you paint without a border. This is why it is important to renew your mind. Faith comes by hearing and hearing by the word of God, be it through reading, listening to audio tapes of the bible, or through good preaching and teaching.

{KJV} {Philippians 2:5} "Let this mind be in you which was also in Christ Jesus:"

{KJV} {Romans 12:2} "And be not conformed to this world: but be ye transformed by the renewing of your mind, that ye may prove what is that good, and acceptable, and perfect, will of God."

{KJV} {Joshua 1:8} "This book of the law shall not depart out of thy mouth; but thou shalt meditate therein day and night, that thou mayest observe to do according to all that is written therein: for then thou shalt make thy way prosperous, and then thou shalt have good success."

{KJV} {Psalms 51:6} "Behold, thou desirest truth in the inward parts: and in the hidden part thou shalt make me to know wisdom."

{KJV} {Romans 10:17} "So then faith cometh by hearing, and hearing by the word of God."

Please answers the questions below on constantly renewing your mind:

{1}. Name some ways how you can constantly renew your mind.

_____

_____

_____

_____

_____

IT'S ALL IN THE
PACKAGE:
PAID IN FULL

{2}. What are some ways that you can protect your mind from negative things?

_____

_____

_____

_____

{3}. Where is the scripture that says I will keep your mind in perfect peace?

_____

_____

{4}. What did you read in the PACKAGE that would prevent or keep you from knowing the word of God?

_____

_____

_____

IT'S ALL IN THE
PACKAGE:
PAID IN FULL

{5}. How can you try to help someone who has a negative mindset about themselves or just life in general?

_____

_____

_____

{6}. What does renew your mind mean to you?

_____

_____

_____

_____

{7}. What is a great tool to renewing your mind spiritually that will never pass away?

_____

_____

_____

IT'S ALL IN THE
PACKAGE:
PAID IN FULL

{8}. Who is responsible for bringing ALL things back to your remembrance once you accept the PACKAGE?

_____

_____

{9}. What is the scripture in the bible that says let this mind be in you, which was also in Christ Jesus?

_____

_____

_____

{10}. What assignment have you abandoned in your life that you know you were called to do?

_____

_____

_____

IT'S ALL IN THE
PACKAGE:
PAID IN FULL

*Reflect on what this chapter means to you?

_____

_____

_____

_____

_____

_____

_____

_____

_____

_____

IT'S ALL IN THE
PACKAGE:
PAID IN FULL

Chapter Nine

THE FAITH OF JESUS BRINGS MANIFESTATION

When we have substance and hope, it is our small vehicle to faith. It is not seen, yet it is us hoping and wishing! Our second vehicle which is faith, is a limousine which is a larger vehicle than our first substance and hope vehicle, which is only a hope and desire not seen yet. Now based on our second vehicle FAITH, a large limousine that has manifested in the natural realm where we can touch it, drive it, see it, possess it, and own it! This stems from our FAITH. It has driven the limousine into manifestation or existence. Faith is simply believing and calling things into existence that already was from the foundation of the world. Remember everything we need IT'S ALL IN THE PACKAGE! GOD HAS PROVIDED ALL! Let me see, I will explain this clearer with my second illustration.

We know faith is the substance of things hoped for; which means you have not seen it yet in the natural realm, and it is not visible to your five natural senses. I want to use an incubator this time. In this illustration YOU are the incubator! Where your substance, hope, and faith reside. It is in its incubation stage, inside of YOU! You are the incubator. Your substance and hope graduates to faith. If I can put it like this. You are like an incubator where substance, hope, and faith reside.

If you remember in a previous chapter when I began to apply myself in the word of God the word began to germinate and grow inside of me, that was the period of gestation. During that stage, I also began to surround myself with men and women of God whose faith was on fire! Faith is contagious so try to be around like-minded faith-filled people. Just like Faith is contagious so is doubt, fear, and unbelief it is contagious also. Stay away from it! It is very crucial to your success in life; just wanted to share that little, chew. So, disassociate yourself from negative unbelieving people, if you can? Short of you needing to minister to them.

Now, back to the incubator which is YOU! Substance, hope, and faith reside within you. God has given every man the measure of faith. Substance, and hope will graduate to faith it's a combo scripture being sowed in your life; from studying and reading the word of God and by confessing what you believe in accordance with the word of God! Now faith brings substance and hope into the visible realm, of what you have been hoping for, at this point and time it is now tangible to you. Where you can see it, touch it, experience it, and even enjoy it; it has now manifested in the visible realm to your natural senses. Now substance and hope has materialized to FAITH! NOW FAITH is ready to deliver from the invisible realm to the visible realm FAITH HAS DELIVERED AND HAS DONE ITS JOB! FAITH CAN DELIVER EVERYTHING THAT'S ALL IN THE PACKAGE!

IT'S MANIFESTO TIME, NOW AMEN!

{KJV} {Hebrews 11:1, 3} "Now faith is the substance of things hoped for, the evidence of things not seen."

"Through faith we understand that the worlds were framed by the word of God, so that things which are seen were not made of things which do appear."

{KJV} {Ephesians 3:20} "Now unto him that is able to do exceeding abundantly above all that we ask or think, according to the power that worketh in us."

{MSG} {Galatians 2:19, 20, 21}

"What actually took place is this: I tried keeping rules and working my head off to please God, and it didn't work. So I quit being a "law man" so that I could be *God's* man." "Christ's life showed me how, and enabled me to do it. I identified myself completely with him. Indeed, I have been crucified with Christ. My ego is no longer central. It is no longer important that I appear righteous before you or have your good opinion, and I am no longer driven to impress God. Christ lives in me. The life you see me living is not mine, but it is lived by faith in the Son of God, who loved me and gave himself for me." "I am not going to go back on that. Is It not clear to you that to go back to that old rule-keeping, peer-pleasing religion would be an abandonment of everything personal and free in my relationship with God? I refuse to do that, to repudiate God's grace.

If a living relationship with God could come by rule-keeping, then Christ died unnecessarily."

{KJV} {Romans 4:16, 17} "Therefore it is of faith, that it might be by grace; to the end the promise might be sure to all the seed; not to that only which is of the law, but to that also which is of the faith of Abraham, who is the father of us all." "(As it is written, I have made thee a father of many nations,) before him whom he believed, even God, who quickeneth the dead, and calleth those things which be not as though they were."

Please answer the 10 questions of faith and manifestation:

{1}. What is faith?

_____

_____

IT'S ALL IN THE PACKAGE:
PAID IN FULL

{2}. Do you have confidence in the faith of God ? (Explain)

_____

_____

_____

_____

{3}. What is the opposite of faith?

_____

_____

_____

_____

{4}. What is the opposite of manifestation?

_____

_____

_____

{5}. Why do you believe that we need faith in this hour, that we live in?

_____

_____

_____

_____

_____

{6}. Write down some of the victories in your life from the results of you trusting and believing God.

_____

_____

_____

_____

_____

IT'S ALL IN THE
PACKAGE:
PAID IN FULL

{7}. What are some of the things that you are hoping for in your life or your families lives that has not materialized yet?

_____

_____

_____

_____

{8}. Do you have areas in your life that gives credence or accredited to you not believing and trusting in God?

_____

_____

_____

_____

_____

IT'S ALL IN THE
PACKAGE:
PAID IN FULL

{9}. What does trusting in God's word mean to you?

_____

_____

_____

_____

{10}. What are some impossible situations in your life that you think are changeless?
THINGS THAT ARE IMPOSSIBLE WITH MAN, ARE POSSIBLE WITH GOD!

_____

_____

_____

_____

Chapter Ten

THE TRUTH WILL MAKE YOU FREE

As I continue, I would like for you to reflect on what you have just read concerning God's written word. God's written word ALWAYS OVERRIDES and SUPERSEDES facts, myths, and statistics or whatever you have heard through the untrue grapevines of this world. I want you to say this aloud "TRUTH ALWAYS OVERRIDES and SUPERSEDES the knowledge of this human world." What I mean by this is, this world's system operates by facts. They have studied that appeals to their natural mind: like doctor's reports, data gathered by man, and their studies according to what they see or what they have acquired through their natural knowledge. God's word of TRUTH ALWAYS OVERRIDES and SUPERSEDES man's facts according to this world's system such as: information, unjust laws, and our judiciary system, limited understanding, and knowledge of the human mind of man. YOU must stand on God's word! You see God's truth is supernatural! You do not deny natural facts; but when it can not change your circumstances according to this world's system, you must stand on God's word to receive different results. In other words, facts or statistics are not the final authority for your life. NOW that we have established that truth, we will continue to walk in it. We will no longer be entangled again with the yoke of bondage and the lies of the enemy, AMEN!

{KJV} {John 8:32} "And ye shall know the TRUTH and the TRUTH shall make you free."

Everything we need has ALREADY been provided in the PACKAGE!

JESUS, GRACE, FAITH, HEALTH, MARRIAGE, CHILDREN, FINANCES, BUSINESS, AND EVERYTHING PERTAINING TO LIFE AND GODLINESS.

In conclusion, we are ending this chapter with questions based on the information you have read thus far.

{1}. What challenges are you facing in your life right NOW?

_____

_____

_____

_____

_____

_____

IT'S ALL IN THE
PACKAGE:
PAID IN FULL

{2}. Do you believe the word of God and trust God, based on the few scriptures I have shared with you in this book?

_____

_____

{3}. What areas in your life have you received negative facts that were not beneficial to your life?

_____

_____

{4}. Have you just been going by man's facts in your life?

_____

_____

_____

{5}. Has the PACKAGE given you hope in hopeless situations in your life to know that God's word of TRUTH has the final authority no matter what it is?

_____

_____

_____

_____

{6}. What does the supernatural mean to you?

_____

_____

_____

_____

IT'S ALL IN THE
PACKAGE:
PAID IN FULL

{7}. Where can you find TRUTH that OVERRIDES negative facts?

_____

_____

_____

_____

{8}. Do you desire inward TRUTH above everything else or others opinions?

_____

_____

_____

_____

_____

{9}. Will you wait on God until the TRUTH manifests or comes to fruition?

_____

_____

IT'S ALL IN THE
PACKAGE:
PAID IN FULL

{10}. Are you willing to share the truth of God's word with others to set them free? (Explain)

_____

_____

_____

_____

We can not leave out the most important part of this book, **"QUALIFICATIONS"** for this PACKAGE is based on the word of God by confession with your mouth, and believing in your heart.

{KJV} {Romans 10: 9, 10}

You just signed for the PACKAGE and received! It is a verbal signature, PRAISE GOD FOR YOUR VICTORY! According to your FAITH be it unto YOU!

NOTHING CAN STOP YOU NOW!

Chapter Eleven

GOD IS FAITHFUL TESTIMONY TIME

{KJV} {Revelation 12:11} "And they overcame him by the blood of the Lamb, and by the word of their testimony; and they loved not their lives unto the death."

Sharing more of my personal testimonies in my life. When I was a child, God healed me from scarlet fever, and tuberculosis. I had nothing to do with it; it was his LOVE, GRACE AND MERCY. I was not saved at the time. Some years later as an adult, He healed me from a thyroid disease. I was placed on Synthroid pills, the brand name was levothyroxine. I was told by the doctors I would be on this medication for life. Not so, God delivered me off that medication. I was also told by a lot of doubting Thomases; if you come off this medicine you will die, but glory be to God I'm still here, that was back in the 80's. God did it again! As my adulthood continued I went to the doctor to see what was going on with my hair and some other ailments in my body. They drew some blood and tried to say I had lupus, within the same week the Doctor's office called me back and said they made a mistake, they had mixed up the wrong blood results. I did NOT HAVE LUPUS; God did it again! The next problem was when I went to see my ob-gyn for an annual routine check up. Fortunately, she scheduled me for a routine mammogram check up. After my mammogram, my results were reviewed by the radiologist. I was called immediately by the Doctor's office to be scheduled for a biopsy, the report looked a little suspicious. I stood on the word of God believing in the faith of Jesus Christ and trusting in Him. During this period, I was determined to stay in peace, not to walk in unforgiveness and not to be in strife, or argue with anyone. I received a call the week of the biopsy, the nurse said, "There is no need to come in for the biopsy." The chief specialist of radiology was in the office that particular day, and took a second look at my results and said I did not need a biopsy. It was not what they thought it was, but God did it again! The next attack was a stroke which was a miracle to me. You see what the enemy meant for a disaster to me, did not work, many are the afflictions, of the righteous; but GOD delivers us out of them ALL! The next attack I encountered was, I had problems with my knees and walking. I went to an Orthopedic Specialist and was told that my cartilages were gone in my knees and was diagnosed with degenerate bone disease. You see, for years I had been walking around in pain. I would have some good days and some bad days. I knew God was a healer, but this time I had in my mind how

IT'S ALL IN THE PACKAGE:
PAID IN FULL

I wanted Him to heal me! After 7 years or more of being in pain, off and on; I was finally convinced by my son and daughter that God was going to bless me by having knee surgery which meant a knee replacement. By this time, I had my own way of how I wanted God to heal me. After all that time, I said, "Ok God I can not tell you how to heal me, I just have to TRUST You." As soon as, I made up my mind to go forth with the surgery; here came another distraction. Before I could have the surgery, I had to be cleared for surgery so I went to my PCP and she scheduled me for the required test that I needed to have the surgery. I went into her office and they did a routine check-up. This nurse practitioner came in and checked my heart and she told me she sensed something wrong and she continued to say, "I guess you will not be having your surgery," needless to say I was livid. Now mind you, it had taken me 7 years or more to reach this place to even have the surgery. So now, my PCP schedules me to go to x-ray to have a CT scan of my chest. By this time, fear was trying to creep in; as a matter of fact, it seemed to me every time I went to that Doctor's office it was a breeding ground for fear! However, the report came back excellent! So from there, my next test was an ultrasound of my heart and the report came back totally positive for me, to be cleared for surgery with no problems. GOD IS SO GOOD and FAITHFUL! So whose report shall we believe? We shall believe the report of the Lord.

{KJV} {1 Peter 2:24} Concerning Health
"Who his own self bare our sins in his own body on the tree, that we, being dead to sins, should live unto righteousness: by whose stripes ye were healed."

{NIV} {Genesis 50: 20, 21} "You intended to harm me, but God intended it for good to accomplish what is now being done, the saving of many lives." "So then, don't be afraid. I will provide for you and your children. And he reassured them and spoke kindly to them."

I have so many more testimonies that I could share with you concerning my children, wealth, shelter, finances, favor, and even in death. As a matter of truth, my whole life! Remember, GOD'S TRUTH the word ALWAYS OVERRIDES AND SUPERSEDES FACTS! But through it all, GOD has ALWAYS BEEN FAITHFUL AND PROVIDED and caused me to be triumphant! There are more scriptures you can read, concerning areas in your life where you have experienced or may never experience God faithfulness. God has been faithful to me in ALL the areas above I mentioned and more. Here are some more scriptures to substantiate the above testimonies. In **Death and Grieving {ESV} {1 Thessalonians 4:13, 14}** "But we do not want you to be uninformed, brothers, about those who are asleep, that you may not grieve as others do who have no hope."

Concerning Lack and Wealth. {BSB} {Psalms 34:10} "Young lions go lacking and hungry, but those who seek the LORD lack no good thing." **{ESV} {Psalms 37:25}** "I have been young, and now am old, yet I have not seen the righteous forsaken or his children begging for bread."

{ESV} {Mathew 6:30, 31, 32, 33} "But if God so clothes the grass of the field, which today is alive and tomorrow is thrown into the oven, will he not much more clothe you, O you of little faith?" "Therefore do not be

IT'S ALL IN THE PACKAGE: PAID IN FULL

anxious," saying, "What shall we eat?" or "What shall we drink?" or "What shall we wear?" "For the Gentiles seek after all these things, and your heavenly Father knows that you need them all." "But seek first the kingdom of God and his righteousness, and all these things will be added to you." Selah!

{KJV} ENDING SCRIPTURES TO STUDY

{**Matthew 9:28, 29**} "And when he was come into the house, the blind men came to him: and Jesus saith unto them, believe ye that I am able to do this? They said unto him, Yea, Lord." "Then touched he their eyes, saying, according to your faith be it unto you."

{**Psalms 107:20**} "He sent his word, and healed them, and delivered them from their destructions."

{**Matthew 24:35**} "Heaven and earth shall pass away, but my words shall not pass away."

{**Isaiah 55:11**} "So shall my word be that goeth forth out of my mouth: it shall not return unto me void, but it shall accomplish that which I please, and it shall prosper in the thing whereto I sent it."

{**Numbers 23:19**} "God is not a man, that he should lie; neither the son of man, that he should repent: Hath he said, and shall he not do it? Or hath he spoken, and shall he not make it good?"

{**Ephesians 3:20**} "Now unto him that is able to do exceeding abundantly above all that we ask or think, according to the power that worketh in us."

{**John 19: 28, 29, 30**} "After this, Jesus knowing that all things were now accomplished, that the scripture might be fulfilled, saith, I thirst." "Now there was set a vessel full of vinegar: and they filled a sponge with vinegar, and put it upon hyssop, and put it to his mouth." "When Jesus therefore had received the vinegar, he said, It is finished: and he bowed his head, and gave up the ghost."

{**Ephesians 6:10, 12, 16, 17**} "Finally, my brethren, be strong in the Lord, and in the power of his might."

"For we wrestle not against flesh and blood, but against principalities, against powers, against the rulers of the darkness of this world, against spiritual wickedness in high places."

"Above all, taking the shield of faith, wherewith ye shall be able to quench all the fiery darts of the wicked."

"And take the helmet of salvation, and the sword of the Spirit, which is the word of God:"

{**Galatians 5:1**} "Stand fast therefore in the liberty wherewith Christ hath made us free, and be not entangled again with the yoke of bondage."

{Proverb 4:20, 21, 22} "My son, attend to my words; Incline thine ear unto my sayings."

"Let them not depart from thine eyes; Keep them in the midst of thine heart."

"For they are life unto those that find them, And health to all their flesh."

{NKJV} {Galatians 2:20} "I have been crucified with Christ; it is no longer I who live, but Christ lives in me; and the life which I now live in the flesh I live by faith in the Son of God, who loved me and gave Himself for me."

IT'S ALL IN THE PACKAGE:
PAID IN FULL

Apostle Para D. Knight is available for conferences, teaching, counseling, prayer, prophecy, and apostolic strategies. She can be reached at {734}-508-2642.

Email: paid.min11@yahoo.com

www.ingramcontent.com/pod-product-compliance
Lightning Source LLC
Chambersburg PA
CBHW071224160426
43196CB00012B/2405